Manifest Like a Misfit

A 30-Day Manifestation Journal

Introduction

Welcome to Manifest Like a Misfit, a no-fluff, soul-deep journal made for the real ones. This 30-day journey is for the beautifully flawed, the misunderstood, the seekers, and the rebels. The ones who are tired of being told to "just think positive" and ready to manifest from a place of truth, not perfection.

Each day is a space for you to reflect, write, affirm, and reclaim your energy. These pages were created for those who feel deeply, carry much, and still dare to want more. The rituals are real. The questions might sting. The magic is already in you. This journal just helps pull it out.

Let's manifest some misfit magic.

Copyright Page

Manifest Like a Misfit: A 30-Day Manifestation
Copyright © 2026 by Char Vernon

First Edition

ISBN: 979-8-9938174-1-5

Published by Char Vernon
Visionary Consults, LLC
www.visionaryconsults.org

For permissions, media inquiries, or bulk orders:
info@visionaryconsults.org

Dedication

This journal is dedicated to my healing journey, not the pretty version, but the real one. The version that required breaking cycles I didn't create, grieving things I never got to fully hold, and finding my way back to a self I didn't always recognize. Every affirmation, every ritual, every page in this book was born from moments where I had to choose myself, even when I didn't feel worthy, even when I didn't feel seen.

It's also dedicated to the spiritual gifts I was born with, the visions, the dreams, the knowing, the protection that I used to question but now trust fully. The things I sense but can't always explain. The way I can feel energy shift in a room. The whispers I get in silence. These gifts have guided me through the dark and reminded me of who I am, even when the world tried to tell me otherwise.

I created this for the parts of me that needed a soft space to land, and for the people reading this who need the same. If you've ever felt like the misfit, the outlier, the one who's always pouring but rarely receiving, I hope these pages feel like a homecoming. This journal isn't just paper and prompts, it's a ritual, a reclamation, a return.

To my spirit.
To my ancestors.
To my purpose.
To my *damn* self.

How to Use This Journal (Without Overthinking It)

This journal wasn't made to be perfect; it was made to be *used*. To get messy, spiritual, honest, and possibly cry a little while manifesting your entire life.

Here's how to move through it like a true misfit:

Start on Day 1.
You can flip to whatever page you want, but this was designed to take you on a full energetic transformation, so start at the top and trust the process.

Light a vibe.
Candle, incense, sage, playlist, or silence. Whatever makes you feel grounded and present. This isn't just journaling. It's rituals.

Do one page a day.
That's it. No pressure to binge. This is sacred, not a sprint.

Speak your affirmations out loud.
Don't just write them. Declare them. Words have power, especially when you say them like you mean them.

Answer honestly.
Don't try to be poetic. Be real. If all you have to say is "I'm tired," write that. Truth moves energy.

Do the rituals when you feel led.
If you don't vibe with one, skip it. If you want to do
it three days in a row, do that. You're the magic.

Use the "Tell Yo' Story" pages to reflect.
These are deeper prompts. Don't rush them. Come
back when your spirit's ready.

Miss a day? Cool. Come back.
Healing isn't linear. This journal will be right here
waiting.

You're not broken.
You're building.
And every page is part of your comeback.

Day 1

Intention for the Day:

What am I calling in today?

What's been holding me back?

How can I reclaim my power today?

Affirmation: I release everything that's not mine to carry, energetically, emotionally, and generationally.

✍ *Freestyle Manifestation:*

(Write your desires like they've already happened.

Brag. Be wild. Be real.)

Day 2

Intention for the Day:

What am I calling in today?

What's been holding me back?

How can I reclaim my power today?

Affirmation: My energy is sacred, and today I reclaim every piece of myself that I gave away for survival.

✍ Freestyle Manifestation:

(Write your desires like they've already happened.

Brag. Be wild. Be real.)

Day 3

Intention for the Day:

What am I calling in today?

What's been holding me back?

How can I reclaim my power today?

Affirmation: I am aligned with protection, peace, and divine order. Nothing formed against me prospers.

Freestyle Manifestation:

(Write your desires like they've already happened.

Brag. Be wild. Be real.)

Day 4

Intention for the Day:

What am I calling in today?

What's been holding me back?

How can I reclaim my power today?

Affirmation: I sweep away spiritual clutter and make room for what's meant for me.

Freestyle Manifestation:

(Write your desires like they've already happened.

Brag. Be wild. Be real.)

Day 5

Intention for the Day:

What am I calling in today?

What's been holding me back?

How can I reclaim my power today?

Affirmation: Even when I've been broken, I rise with purpose. My story isn't over, it's just getting good.

(Write your desires like they've already happened.

Brag. Be wild. Be real.)

Day 6

Intention for the Day:

What am I calling in today?

What's been holding me back?

How can I reclaim my power today?

Affirmation: I am connected to a higher power, rooted in truth, and guided by intuition.

Freestyle Manifestation:

(Write your desires like they've already happened.

Brag. Be wild. Be real.)

Day 7

Intention for the Day:

What am I calling in today?

What's been holding me back?

How can I reclaim my power today?

Affirmation: My magic isn't always pretty but it's powerful, and it's mine.

Freestyle Manifestation:
(Write your desires like they've already happened.
Brag. Be wild. Be real.)

Day 8

Intention for the Day:

What am I calling in today?

What's been holding me back?

How can I reclaim my power today?

Affirmation: I deserve ease without explanation. My peace is not up for negotiation.

Freestyle Manifestation:
(Write your desires like they've already happened.
Brag. Be wild. Be real.)

Day 9

Intention for the Day:

What am I calling in today?

What's been holding me back?

How can I reclaim my power today?

Affirmation: I trust divine timing, even when I don't understand divine detours.

🌿 *Freestyle Manifestation:*

(Write your desires like they've already happened.

Brag. Be wild. Be real.)

Day 10

Intention for the Day:

What am I calling in today?

What's been holding me back?

How can I reclaim my power today?

Affirmation: I am magnetic to opportunities that match my worth, not my wounds.

Freestyle Manifestation:
(Write your desires like they've already happened.
Brag. Be wild. Be real.)

Day 11

Intention for the Day:

What am I calling in today?

What's been holding me back?

How can I reclaim my power today?

Affirmation: My voice matters, and today, I speak life into my own dreams.

Freestyle Manifestation:

(Write your desires like they've already happened.

Brag. Be wild. Be real.)

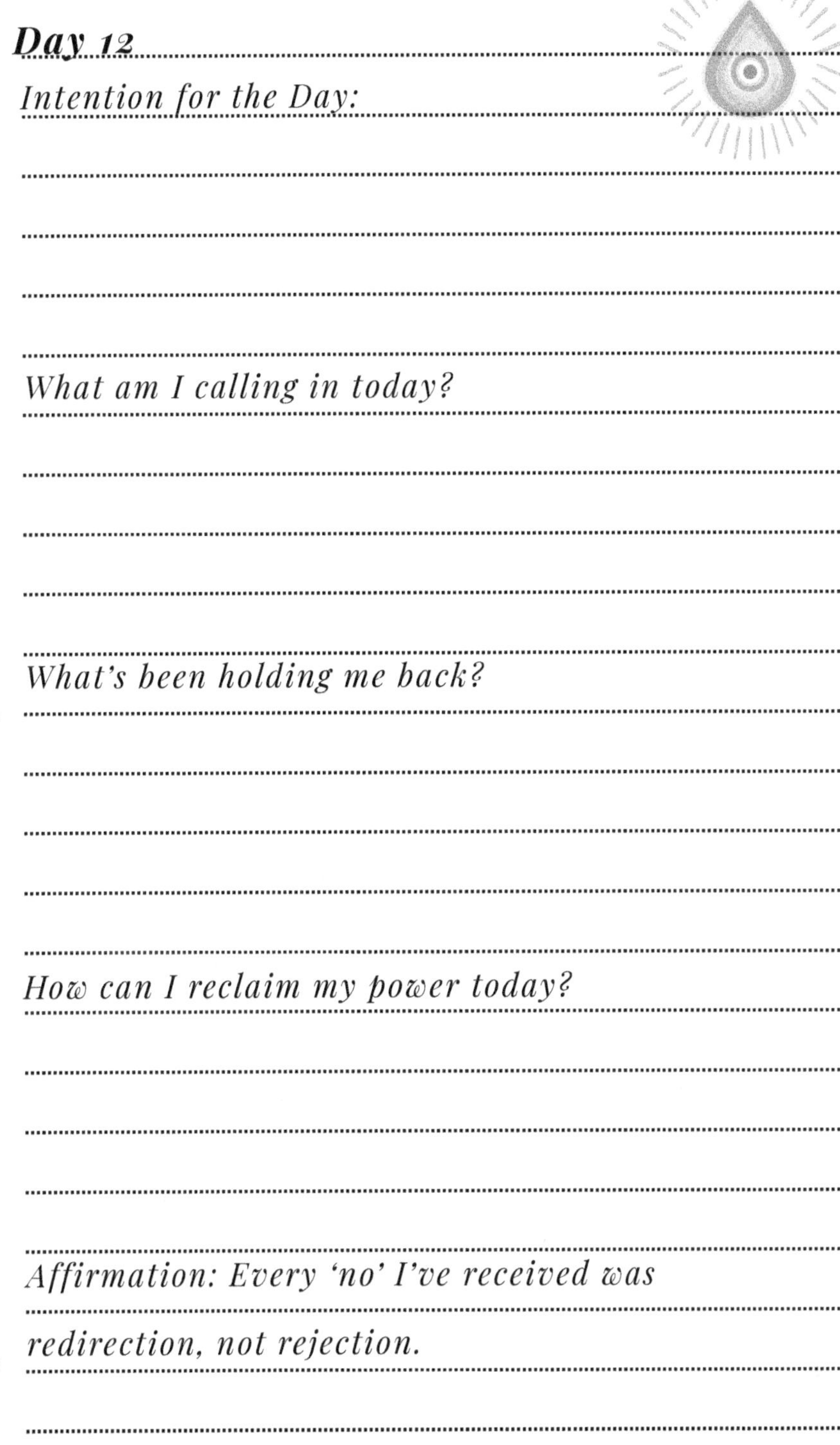

Day 12

Intention for the Day:

What am I calling in today?

What's been holding me back?

How can I reclaim my power today?

Affirmation: Every 'no' I've received was redirection, not rejection.

🌿 *Freestyle Manifestation:*

(Write your desires like they've already happened.

Brag. Be wild. Be real.)

Day 13

Intention for the Day:

What am I calling in today?

What's been holding me back?

How can I reclaim my power today?

Affirmation: I forgive myself for shrinking to survive. I expand to thrive.

🍃 *Freestyle Manifestation:*

(Write your desires like they've already happened.

Brag. Be wild. Be real.)

Day 14
Intention for the Day:

What am I calling in today?

What's been holding me back?

How can I reclaim my power today?

Affirmation: My path may be different, but it's divinely designed just for me.

Freestyle Manifestation:

(Write your desires like they've already happened.

Brag. Be wild. Be real.)

Day 15
Intention for the Day:

What am I calling in today?

What's been holding me back?

How can I reclaim my power today?

Affirmation: I let go of comparison. I am not behind, I am becoming.

Freestyle Manifestation:

(Write your desires like they've already happened.

Brag. Be wild. Be real.)

Day 16
Intention for the Day:

What am I calling in today?

What's been holding me back?

How can I reclaim my power today?

Affirmation: I walk with ancestors whose names I know and those I don't, and they protect me.

Freestyle Manifestation:

(Write your desires like they've already happened.

Brag. Be wild. Be real.)

Day 17

Intention for the Day:

What am I calling in today?

What's been holding me back?

How can I reclaim my power today?

Affirmation: My manifestations don't need to look perfect. They need to feel aligned.

Freestyle Manifestation:

(Write your desires like they've already happened.

Brag. Be wild. Be real.)

Day 18

Intention for the Day:

What am I calling in today?

What's been holding me back?

How can I reclaim my power today?

Affirmation: I deserve money, miracles, and moments of stillness all at once.

🪶 *Freestyle Manifestation:*

(Write your desires like they've already happened.

Brag. Be wild. Be real.)

Day 19

Intention for the Day:

What am I calling in today?

What's been holding me back?

How can I reclaim my power today?

Affirmation: I honor the divine in me, even on the days I feel a mess.

🖋 Freestyle Manifestation:

(Write your desires like they've already happened.

Brag. Be wild. Be real.)

Day 20

Intention for the Day:

What am I calling in today?

What's been holding me back?

How can I reclaim my power today?

Affirmation: I show up for myself today like I would for someone I love.

Freestyle Manifestation:
(Write your desires like they've already happened.
Brag. Be wild. Be real.)

Day 21

Intention for the Day:

....

....

....

....

What am I calling in today?

....

....

....

....

What's been holding me back?

....

....

....

....

How can I reclaim my power today?

....

....

....

....

Affirmation: My intuition is louder than fear and clearer than doubt.

....

Freestyle Manifestation:

(Write your desires like they've already happened.

Brag. Be wild. Be real.)

....

....

....

....

....

....

....

....

....

....

....

....

....

Write your desires like they've already happened.

Day 22

Intention for the Day:

What am I calling in today?

What's been holding me back?

How can I reclaim my power today?

Affirmation: I bless my home, my name, and my goals with sacred intention.

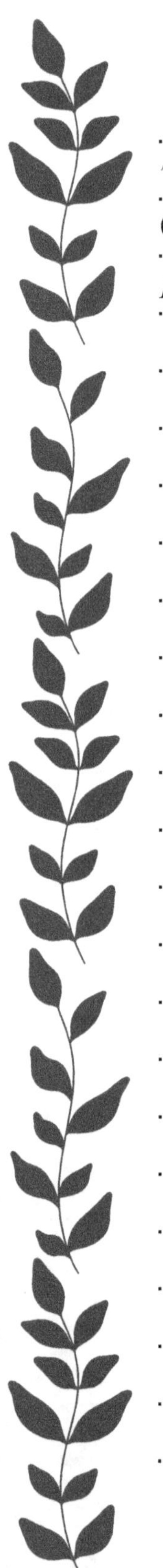

✿ Freestyle Manifestation:

(Write your desires like they've already happened.

Brag. Be wild. Be real.)

Day 23

Intention for the Day:

What am I calling in today?

What's been holding me back?

How can I reclaim my power today?

Affirmation: I am proof that healing doesn't have to look holy. It just has to feel honest.

Freestyle Manifestation:

(Write your desires like they've already happened.

Brag. Be wild. Be real.)

Day 24

Intention for the Day:

What am I calling in today?

What's been holding me back?

How can I reclaim my power today?

Affirmation: I make room for unexpected blessings because I'm no longer blocking them with disbelief.

Freestyle Manifestation:

(Write your desires like they've already happened.

Brag. Be wild. Be real.)

Day 25

Intention for the Day:

What am I calling in today?

What's been holding me back?

How can I reclaim my power today?

Affirmation: I manifest from the soul, not from desperation.

Freestyle Manifestation:

(Write your desires like they've already happened.

Brag. Be wild. Be real.)

Day 26

Intention for the Day:

What am I calling in today?

What's been holding me back?

How can I reclaim my power today?

Affirmation: I honor rest as a radical form of resistance and renewal.

Freestyle Manifestation:
(Write your desires like they've already happened.
Brag. Be wild. Be real.)

Day 27

Intention for the Day:

What am I calling in today?

What's been holding me back?

How can I reclaim my power today?

Affirmation: My boundaries are love in action, and they're non-negotiable.

🌿 *Freestyle Manifestation:*

(Write your desires like they've already happened.

Brag. Be wild. Be real.)

Day 28

Intention for the Day:

What am I calling in today?

What's been holding me back?

How can I reclaim my power today?

Affirmation: I carry the resilience of my bloodline and the rebirth of my own becoming.

Freestyle Manifestation:
(Write your desires like they've already happened.
Brag. Be wild. Be real.)

Day 29

Intention for the Day:

What am I calling in today?

What's been holding me back?

How can I reclaim my power today?

Affirmation: The Universe doesn't skip misfits; it saves the boldest blessings for us.

Freestyle Manifestation:

(Write your desires like they've already happened.

Brag. Be wild. Be real.)

Day 30

Intention for the Day:

What am I calling in today?

What's been holding me back?

How can I reclaim my power today?

Affirmation: I am the spell. I am the answer. I am the moment.

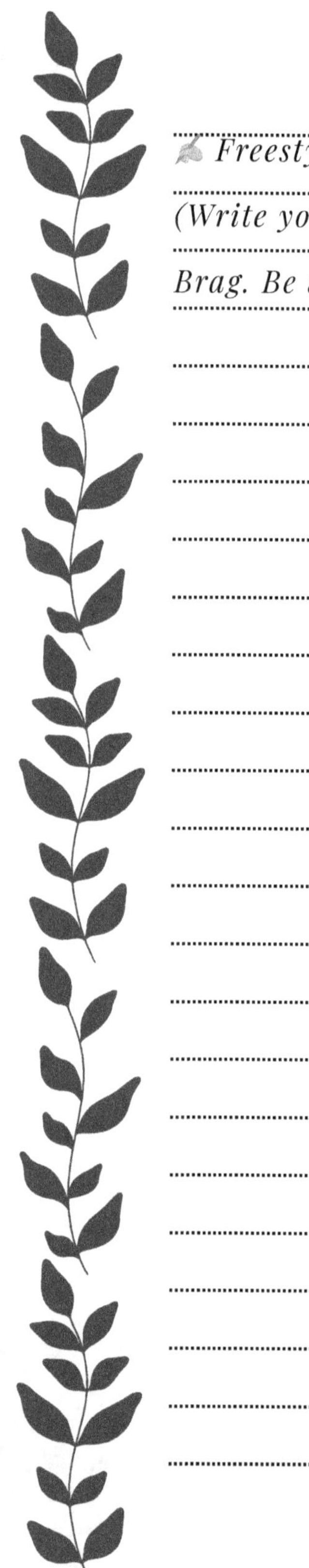

🌿 *Freestyle Manifestation:*

(Write your desires like they've already happened.

Brag. Be wild. Be real.)

Sprinkle A little Spiritual Misfit Spice

These rituals are light, positive, and rooted in ancestral wisdom. You don't need to be an expert, just intentional.

🌿 Road Opening Candle: Dress an orange candle with olive oil and sprinkle a pinch of cinnamon. Burn it while speaking aloud what you want unblocked (e.g., finances, energy, love).

🧂 Salt & Vinegar Floor Wash: Mix Sea salt, apple cider vinegar, and warm water. Mop your space (or wipe down your front door) to clear negativity and welcome fresh energy.

🕯 Ancestor Light: Light a white candle on a plate with a glass of water beside it. Speak gratitude to your ancestors and ask for clarity or blessings.

💰 Money-Drawing Oil: Mix cinnamon, clove, and a touch of honey with almond or grapeseed oil. Anoint your wallet, cash, or even your journal pages.

◎ Protection Jar: Fill a small jar with black salt, garlic peel, rosemary, and a protective sigil or symbol. Keep it near your front door or workspace.

About the Author

Char Vernon is an author, HR professional, and creative entrepreneur with over 15 years of experience in human resources, executive support, and workforce strategy. She holds a Master's degree in Human Resource Management and is currently pursuing her Doctorate in Communications, combining real-world expertise with advanced academic insight.

As the founder of Visionary Consults, LLC, Char creates practical tools, career resources, and engaging content designed to empower individuals to navigate both professional and personal challenges with confidence.

Her body of work spans multiple genres, from workforce development guides like 2025 is a Shhh Show: The Struggles in Today's Job Market* to imaginative children's books such as Brandon's Brave Biking Bonanza. Her children's stories blend rhythm, creativity, and life lessons, encouraging resilience, critical thinking, and confidence in young readers.

From her first publication to a growing catalog of books and resources, Char's work reflects continuous growth, authenticity, and a commitment to creating meaningful, impactful content.